D0699711

Dear Parrot

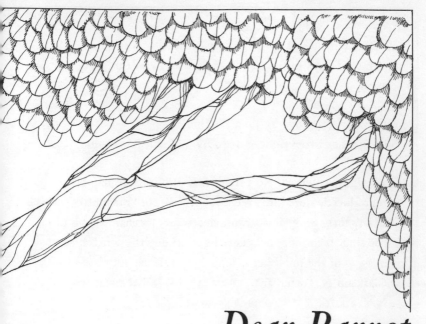

Dear Parrot

*Pertaining to the care,
nurture &
befriending of man's oldest pet*

BY JOHN PHILLIPS

Illustrations by
WILLIAM BRAMHALL

CLARKSON N. POTTER, INC.
PUBLISHERS, NEW YORK
Distributed by Crown Publishers

Published simultaneously in Canada by General Publishing Company Limited
First edition
Printed in the United States of America

Library of Congress Cataloging in Publication Data

Phillips, John, 1924–
    Dear parrot.

    1. Parrots. I Bramhall, William. II. Title.
SF473.P3P44   636.6'865   79–9075
ISBN 0–517–53868–7

The author's theories on the Parrot are very much—indeed, exclusively—his own, drawn from a timeless intimacy with a remarkable bird. The reader, whether equally familiar with the Parrot or making his first acquaintance in these pages, may balk at certain of the author's assertions. Mr. Phillips, nonetheless, will not retract a word of his disquisition. It is based less on banal fact than on Subjective Truth, which—in the tradition of other profound and rueful, if egocentric, thinkers—the author insists is all that matters.

To Suay

She could always see it from the Parrot's point of view.

Dear Parrot

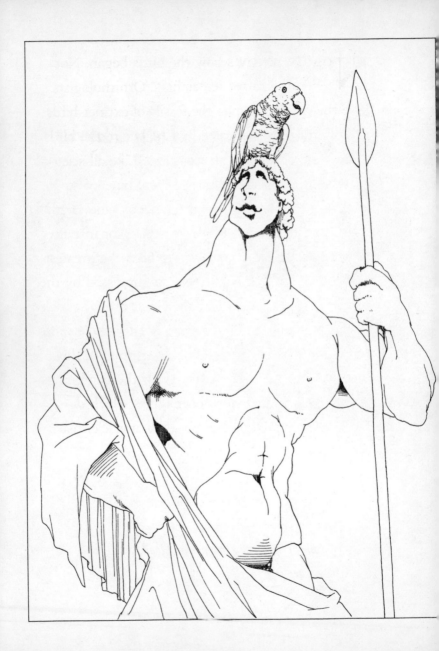

NOBODY KNOWS how the birds began. Not even the Parrot remembers. Ornithologists base their theories upon the fossils of extinct birds and of creatures that came in time before the birds —eons and eitons and alautons ago. Like all scientists, ornithologists are learned men, but not so wise as the philosophers and the poets, who taught the scientists what to think. Aristotle, for instance, the ancient Greek who may have been the greatest thinker who ever thought, was so impressed by the parrots his pupil Alexander the Great brought back from the conquest of India some twenty-three centuries ago that he wrote a fine description of this bird for future ornithologists. As for the beginnings of life on earth, here are a poet's lines which describe them more intriguingly than any scientist has done:

> *When fishes flew and forests walked*
> *And figs grew upon thorn,*
> *One night when the moon was blood,*
> *Then surely I was born.*

That is from a poem about the Donkey. He resembles the Parrot only in that ignorant people have made both the subjects of tiresome jokes. A smaller relative of the Horse, the Donkey has ears that are supposed to be too long for his head and his head too long for the rest of him and therefore he has been considered funny or strange or weird. That could explain why the poet makes the Donkey's birth under a blood-red moon seem like Halloween. Nowadays figs grow on trees, but the Parrot remembers when figs grew on thorny bushes and it was difficult to eat one. Back in the Jurassic period the forests didn't actually walk, of course. Sometimes it *looked* as if the forests were walking— or, anyhow, jumping around a bit—because they were full of dinosaurs and brontosauruses roaring about and knocking down the trees.

That Brontosaurus was a lizardlike beast, about as long as a middle-sized airliner and as heavy. If you visit a natural history museum, look for a reconstructed skeleton of the Brontosaurus or for a replica in plastic large as life with his eyes and

gigantic mouth grinning down upon you. Think: when this animal roamed the earth he made a roar like thunder, and the oldtime Greeks, who must have learned about him from their prehistoric ancestors, named him Brontosaurus, which meant Thunder Lizard. He ate trees. His jaws were big enough to hold a rubber tree without much trouble; his teeth were sharp as spears and big as fire hydrants. He waddled through the primordial forests and just chomped on trees when he got hungry. Picture a herd of twenty or thirty Thunder Lizards slouching along with their mouths full of broad-leaved trees which they have pulled out of the ground, roots and all. No wonder it looked as though the forests walked. That's what the poet meant and what the Parrot saw, the first Parrot, for surely he was there among the fishes that flew.

Not the flying fishes we know that skim over the tropic waves—fishes that really flew over the land, the jungles, and the rain forests. Most ornithologists believe the birds were reptiles or scaly fishlike snaky things that lived in the ocean until they crawled ashore and learned to fly. Ornithologists believe that uncountable centuries ago when these reptiles began to be birds they turned their scales into feathers.

THE PARROT, like any other bird, still keeps his scales upon his feet. Should you have the luck and the good taste to have a pet parrot of your own, he won't mind your examining his feet. The Parrot has been on earth so long that he is closer than most birds to the reptile, and this must be why he is so smart: he knows the secrets of the tortoise. If you invite your parrot to perch on your wrist, his leathery toes upon your skin will feel a trifle snakelike. If he and you are the friends you should be and you really trust each other, he will snakestep his way along your outstretched arm and perch upon your shoulder. Probably the Parrot's favorite spot is upon his friend's shoulder. While he's there you may take a close look at the bright little feathers that grow in delicate layers ever littler as they near his eye. The patterns of these feathers, each so intricately placed to overlap another, are the patterns of the scales of a fish.

Doubtless your parrot likes to have his head scratched. He will lower his head, rest his beak on your shoulder and close his eyes in rapture as you gently scratch. Nothing, not even a mate to share his lonely cage, gives a tame parrot more pleasure. He will puff up his neck feathers so you may run your finger through his undercoat of downy feathers and bristling tiny pinfeathers. When the Parrot molts and renews his plumage, the old feathers drop out and the tightly rolled pinfeathers sprout and unfurl as ferns do and exactly where they belong in the feather pattern. It's something like and yet a lot more complicated than the way a child's new teeth replace old ones.

Instead of teeth the Parrot does his biting with

a strong, curved beak. He does not chew his meal of fruits and greens and seeds; he grinds it down with grains of sand or gravel he stores in a compartment of his throat known as his crop. A tame and trusting parrot will eat right from your mouth. Place on your lip a sunflower seed, making the correct parrot noises as you do so. The courtly bird, who could easily with a careless thrust of that sharp beak mangle your lip, will pick up the seed so softly you hardly notice it.

Offer him a peanut roasted in its shell and a parrot accepts it with his foot. The foot becomes a hand and his toes fingers to hold the peanut while he munches it, the way you'd eat a cookie. (If you know another bird that can do this trick, I'd like to meet him.) The Parrot breaks the peanut shell and while his thick black tongue spews shell fragments on your shoulder, he nonchalantly swallows the nut. He offers no apology for the mess; he knows it's the natural thing to do. In his tranquil fashion he will chomp up a carrot or a celery stalk; he will demolish a pencil or any other wooden beaksharpener, and the shreds and splinters will drift down onto your carpet as if it were the rain forest's floor. It is the same with old feathers he plucks out while molting, the same with his excretory functions which he indulges whenever the urge is on him, no matter what he splatters with his wet green and white droppings, or whom.

The scaly feet are fine for perching, too—for holding tight to a branch during a tropical storm—and for climbing. The Parrot is yoke-toed: two toes point forward and two behind. His beak serves as a third hand when he climbs a tree or a vine in the wild or, in captivity, a rope. In your own parlor he will climb just as efficiently up an upholstered sofa or a curtain to the very top, hitching himself up there with beak and toes.

Those feet are very bad for doing just one thing and that is walking; they simply weren't designed for pedestrian use. The Parrot loses all his style when he must move flat-footed across a floor with a slightly foolish rocking of the body. The claws that dig so well into cloth or a tree's bark

only encumber him on a horizontal surface. He cannot scamper like a sandpiper or waddle like a web-footed duck. The best he can manage is a droll flock-flocking walk as his curved claws strike and slide uselessly on the boards.

Sometimes when he's out of his cage and feeling at loose ends, a house parrot flock-flocks his solitary way down the corridors, searching for his friend. His eyes are keen but since they are set on either side of his head, he cannot see in front of him. To find out where he's going he has to turn his head to and fro, using one eye and then the other. When he comes to an open door, he cocks his head sideways to see if his friend is in the room. To make his presence felt he will commence to bite at his friend's shoe or subtly nip his ankle. He wants up on the shoulder: to make this perfectly clear he may well dance and shuffle a foot or two from side to side and fan out his tailfeathers. That's what he used to do in the rain forest to impress his mate with the elegance of his plumage. He keeps on with the parrot dance from side to side and

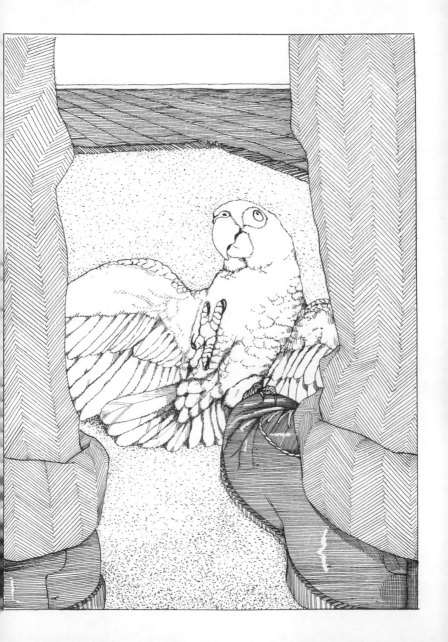

cocks his head up at his friend. Now the pupils of his eyes shrink and dilate in black dots centered in the yellow circle of the iris. The black expands and contracts upon the yellow so wildly the effect is fairly psychedelic. This is the Parrot's way of winking at you and an important part of the whole performance that ornithologists call the courtship display. All of this activity is accompanied by a serenade of clucks, whistles, laughs, and croaks that only say *Pay attention to me. I want up on your shoulder.*

WHY ALL THE FUSS? Why doesn't the bird just fly onto the shoulder? If he's a healthy bird and his wings aren't clipped, why won't he fly? Because when a parrot gets used to a cage he loses the habit of flying. There is no excuse for the wicked practice of clipping a bird's wings and no reason for doing this to a bird born in an aviary roomy enough for a number of birds to fly around in and pretend they are free. Often an aviary contains trees or imitation trees with hollow trunks for the Parrot to nest in as he is accustomed to do in the wild. Captive birds have to lay their eggs somewhere and they use these contrivances, which do not fool the Parrot one minute. Still he is an adaptable bird and plucky; he has the pride of his ancestors, he refuses to feel sorry for himself. He finds solace in knowing some parrots have lived more than one hundred years in captivity, and that is a lot longer than human beings who put him there.

A tame parrot flies the swift, direct flight of his brothers that dart through the tops of the rain forests. He is lazy, though, about flying; he had rather ride around on his friend's shoulder or even flock-flock along the floor than fly. The reasons he uses his wings at all are instinctive: A) he feels neglected and wants attention; B) he loses his grip while climbing; C) a sudden noise, no more than popcorn popping, startles him and he takes to the

air. The time to tell for sure that you are a parrot's friend is when the panicked bird is flying about the room in search of a safe perch and you stretch out your arm and he lands on it.

Out of doors it is risky to uncage a parrot. He is eager to explore the shady branches of a tree and expects to clamber back down again to his friend. But what if a branch snaps off in the wind? If a robin is startled he flies off to safety with other robins. A parrot startled in a backyard in Seattle or a rooftop in Chicago can only fly off into danger, and he will find no parrots there.

The North American weather is tough on a tropical bird. If he belongs to the great family of Amazon parrots, his basic jungle green that camouflaged him in the rain forest does not blend well with the snow. He isn't a penguin; an African or a Latin background has not equipped him to survive our winters and he too easily expires of enteritis or pneumonia; a summer's cold hailstorm can do him in too.

Only a gallant exception like the Monk Parakeet thrives in bad weather: a smaller cousin of the Parrot, he comes from Argentina where the weather can be icy indeed. A few winters back some of these parakeets escaped in New York City—or were set loose on purpose by their coldhearted owners. Far from expiring in the coldest winters New York has ever known, the Monks have nested and hatched until now their flocks are seen in all five boroughs of the city. If this business keeps up, the Monk Parakeet could replace the pigeon as boss bird of New York.

Now and then you read in the papers about a parrot who flies to a high place and will not be coaxed down. Firemen come with fire ladders, but parrots don't use fire ladders. On May 26, 1978, a blazing Red Macaw—who is another cousin of the Parrot but twice his size—would not aban-

Jellicoe City Bann

May 27, 1978

Exotic Bird Rescued
School Teacher Is Heroine

JELLICOE CI
Red Macaw bel
M. Rowe escap
yesterday and f
five hours frus
by police and f
rescue. The bird
mistakenly iden
"Roger" but lat
as "Rajah" flew
a linden tree. E
and state troope
unsuccessful un
was spotted by
children who ar
fifth grade clas
by Mrs. Rowe. T
by whistling a
as Mrs. Rowe, h
a tidy bun, clim
ladder and took
Macaw, which is
to the Parrot, on
as bystanders c

'I don't know
would have don
hadn't showed
Chester Doozle
firechief. He sa
"great courage"
the fireladder
on her shoulder
while it whistle
Too Old to Drea
taught by Mrs. R
favorite song.
Everyone agree
whistled beaut

DRAMA IN THE TREETOPS occurs as Mrs. Effie M. Rowe, of this city, extri-
cates her pet Macaw from the branches of a linden tree.

don a linden tree in Jellicoe City, Indiana. He would
not come down for the Fire Department, not for
the Police Department, or the state troopers, who
were all calling to him, "Roger, Roger, won't you
please come down?" This vain effort persisted
until midafternoon, when school let out. Some pass-
ing fifth-graders noticed the glorious long-tailed
bird. "Lookit!" they yelled. "It's Rajah." Straight-
away the macaw responded by whistling a poi-
gnant melody that charmed all ears.

The fifth-graders knew his name was Rajah
and not Roger because he belonged to their home-
room teacher, a kindly widow named Effie M.
Rowe. Mrs. Rowe wears her silver hair in a tidy
bun and she has a lovely smile. Though she looks
a bit plump to have climbed to the top of a fire
ladder and carried Rajah home on her shoulder,
that's just what she did. Next morning she and
Rajah had their picture in the Jellicoe City *Banner*.
It was Mrs. Rowe, the *Banner* states in its brief
account, who taught Rajah to whistle "When I
Grow Too Old to Dream," which is her favorite song.

All parrots can whistle but not all can carry a tune. Most any parrot can produce the shrill sound of a sailor whistling at a pretty girl what once we called the "Wolf Whistle." It takes an uncommonly gifted and accomplished bird to render an air so exquisite as Mrs. Rowe's favorite. *When I grow too old to dream, your kiss will live in my heart.* . . . How sweet a song. A long, long time ago Mrs. Rowe must have sung it to Mr. Rowe, when they were courting. She must have sung it a lot and the song billowed from her comfortable bosom in a rolling contralto until Mr. Rowe—a young man with, I am certain, clean hands and a pure heart—implored her: "Effie, dear heart. Effie, will you be my wife?" I am sure Rajah has listened to the widow Rowe humming the tune through so many a solitary evening that by now it just whistles itself.

It is well that Rajah never aspired to *sing* the song. At least I trust he did not. Canaries can sing but they cannot whistle and they seldom try. Parrots can whistle but they cannot sing, though they far too freely try to. Once a parrot is moved to song, he squawks and screeches; he can screech a screech as nervewracking as the Peacock's. If you can't close your ears to the sound, it helps to remember the Parrot means to sing as beautifully as the canary or the meadowlark, and he actually thinks he can. This is the biggest mistake the Parrot makes. You just have to forgive him for it. Try to look at the problem from the Parrot's point of view.

Screeching and squawking, after all, are as much a part of the jungle sound track as the trumpeting of elephants and the nattering of monkeys. To the Parrot they are joyous halloos to inform the flock he is feeling tiptop and proud to be a parrot. In the rain forest the most active times of his day are also the most raucous: when the flock departs at dawn for the day's feeding, and again at dusk while it settles down for the night, there is a great beating of wings and jostling of branches and parrots call out to each other. Thousands of miles away, alone in a cage, the captive parrot remembers.

So it is that the first thing in the morning, as he hears the sounds of a waking household, this parrot squawks. He means, *I'm a parrot, pay attention to me.* When night falls he squawks at the first noise of his friend returning home, and he will scold you if you don't give the proper greeting. He will scold you if you do not open the cage and let him up on your shoulder, so that you both may sit a while and calm the day's passion. If you will only do this, he will make nothing louder than satisfaction sounds while he preens his feathers. In a grateful impulse he will preen his friend's hair too. Softly he processes your locks in his beak, a few strands at a time, to make sure they are free of mites and cooties. If you have just had a shower-bath, he will help dry you by squeezing drops of water from your hair or your whiskers. In the contemplative silence all you can hear is his upper bill scraping upon the lower. He yawns perhaps or drops his head for a goodnight scratch. Back in the cage he perches on one foot, the other clenched

into a yoke-toed fist: he relaxes his quill muscles and the feathers puff out, giving a slight potbelly but at the same time ennobling his profile so that it resembles a postage-stamp figure of the national bird of some emergent Caribbean nation. He is waiting for you to turn out the light and return him to his jungle dreams.

Sleep—in moderation always and only in its due nocturnal course—comes easily to the Parrot. He prefers, of course, to relish the caress of Hypnos while poised erect and one-legged on his perch. Still, he will make a concession now and then, if that will relieve another's insomnia. The aspect of a slumbering parrot, his eyelids shut and feathers puffed, can have a sedative effect. Sometimes a sleepless friend succumbs to an insidious instinct to take his bird to bed and just cork off there beside him, parrot-style.

Only for this friend would the Parrot endure the inconvenience and the quintessentially unbird-worthy posture of lying on his back, wings folded, beak to the ceiling, yoke toes gripping the bed sheet. It's a chore. He will yawn and shut his eyes; he will feign snoozing until he hears the first sure sound of a snore. Human snoring, he feels, releases him from sham and frees him to reindulge his parrot nature. So he turns belly-down and snakes underneath the covers. It's dark down there and soft. The bedclothes upon his head are no heavier than banana leaves and, now snakestepping sideways, now flocking forward, he makes his way through the tunnel of cloth as through a hollow tree while he investigates its potentials for a roost. Cluck-clucking to himself in pleasant cadences, he proceeds from shoulder to toe the length of his sleeping bed mate. All the while his scrupulous beak eschews the temptations to nip, tweak, and bedevil the tender epidermis which is lying wholly at its mercy. There are much worse sleeping companions than the Parrot; you can bet on that.

It is perfectly correct to sleep with the Parrot. Let's emphasize this. *There are no sinister implications to this practice and no unseemly inferences; it is okay.* (Granted the Parrot is not fastidious about his droppings,

nonetheless this mutual sleep can be—at least most of the time, if not pushed beyond its limits and if easily laundered drip-dry bed linen is in supply— quite decently hygienic.)

Fresh in the morning the friend awakes. His bird could be reposing puffed-up upon the pillow, having abandoned the bed roost during the night, knowing it's healthier to sleep in fresh air. The curved beak opens wide and shows the black tongue; the yawn is performed and the wings are stretched separately, one after the other. Perhaps long back in the rain forest this was the hour he particularly enjoyed to bathe. If so and if his friend likes a shower before breakfast, fine and dandy. All that's needed is a steamy bathroom, moisture dripping from the tiles. The idea is to simulate if not the rain forest at least the humidity there. A wooden towel rack will serve as a bathing perch, or a kitchen chair—something that can take the wet and be placed close to the shower bath.

By slow, deliberate flicks of wrist and fingers the first tentative drops of warm water are cast upon the bird. If he hates this, if it scares him, he will squawk and fly away. Or he will hold fast, commence to flap his wings, and burble with delight in a homemade tropic rain. He flaps and squawks and fans his tail for more rain, more. Hand splashes and cupped hands full of water may never be enough. Then it is feasible to lean one's back directly into and against the shower stream and—fiendish, perhaps, but good clean fun just the same —to deflect the spray at steepening angles and increasing force upon the plumed partner in this ecstatic water sport.

Finally there is no dry towel, no absorbent surface left within square yards of the downpour. The perch stands in a splashing pond that was the bathroom floor. Its raucous occupant, feathers drenched and darkly sodden now and piteously sticking to scrawny clavicle and sternum and ribs and with disquieting resemblance to a plucked and oven-ready fowl, *persists* with wings at full stretch, kitelike, to demand more rain. He has become an avatar, an insatiate jungle rain god. You have to remove him to the sunshine, let the feathers dry as he shakes out the water and spruces them and refreshes their noble colors for a new day.

CERTAIN PEOPLE see a parrot and immediately ask, "Does it talk?" They loom over the unhappy bird and repeat the old imbecilic question, "Polly want a cracker?" No sophisticated bird will tolerate so old hat a name as that one, and the Parrot is nothing if not sophisticated. And to be called "it" is a flagrant insult: there are Male and Female parrots, cocks and hens, but, unlike chickens, they cannot be distinguished by their size and feathers. Among most Amazon species and the African Gray, male and female have the same dimensions and, where plumage is concerned, they are positively unisex. Their owners can only guess at their pets' sexes and they must always be prepared for a surprise. A parrot that for years was known as Harry may very well lay an egg in his cage one night and thereby change his name to Harriet.

Certain people don't understand parrots at all. "Does Polly talk?" they go on saying. "Hello, Polly. Pretty Polly." They stick their fingers into the cage and poke him as if he were a taxidermist's specimen. That scares him and he makes an angry noise; they poke again and then the parrot bites as hard as he can. His beak is his protection and he keeps it sharp enough to bite a finger to the bone. A tame parrot that is exposed to strangers who bedevil him does not stay tame for long.

The world knows the best-talking parrot is the African Gray. His head and neck are narrower and remind you more of his reptilian ancestors than his fuller-faced green cousins from South America. His wings and body are pale gray and slate gray and his tail feathers a vermilion red—almost the colors of the Confederacy. He comes from Kenya and Tanzania and the slopes of mysterious Kiliman-

jaro, a mountain half as old as time. The Gray is at
ease in all earthly and celestial tongues and has a
mind-boggling repertory of sounds. A baby crying,
a lady laughing. Hounds on a summer's night, a
mile away, baying at the moon. Sneezing. Cough-
ing. Burping. Snoring. It's almost spooky, the way
the Gray associates sight with sound. He sees you
reach for your handkerchief and he makes the
sound of you blowing your nose before you can.
Put a drinking glass under a faucet and he does the
splashing of water before a drop of water has
splashed.

If you speak directly to a parrot, any parrot,
he's apt to cock his head and silently stare you
down. He doesn't care a whit what you are telling
him; he may be mildly interested in the sound of
your voice. He understands what you're saying all
too well: *Good morning, Polly is a pretty bird*, and the
rest. Merely he finds this patter unworthy of reply;
so he stares at you and measures your voice. Later,
when you are some distance off, perhaps in another
room with your mind on other things, then of a

sudden he will repeat to you distinctly and diabolically in imitation of your voice the silly things you told him. He does this quite simply to demonstrate the imbecility with which people treat parrots, how generally banal and empty he finds human converse. Happily he would discuss with you those human ideas which interest him, such as the Binomial Theorem or the Sermon on the Mount, but nobody asks him about these.

There are grown-up men and women so intent on heaping junktalk on their birds that they stay hours at a time by a cage in the dark so the parrot must listen without distraction as they repeat their mindless slogans. They expect this discriminating bird to memorize their twaddlement and say it back word for word—or "parrot" it, as we condescendingly say. Some so-called parrot fanciers go so far as to purchase phonograph records—masterpieces of junktalk, vapid and treacly sayings spoken by a vapid person in a treacly voice. *Good morning! How are you this morning? I am such a pretty bird. Have a good day. . . .* You and I can always seize this horrible record and throw it out the window. The parrot can't. Caged and shut up in a dark room with this rot repeating in his ears, as if he weren't captive enough already, he has to be a captive audience too.

At least the record doesn't teach him cuss words, you say. How come parrots say cuss words?... Because they're forever hearing people say them. Through the millennia, in the ancient and the recent tongues, the Parrot has heard these words. The Parrot says our cuss words for the same reason he says any words: to show how ridiculous we sound.

FEW THEY ARE and greatly prized, but there is an elite corps of parrots who refuse to play the talk game. They will not talk junktalk, or cuss, or condescend to any other form of human converse.

Whoever hopes to communicate with this superlative bird must use the language of the Parrot, which is elaborate beyond our comprehending. It is at once inflectional and polytonic, monosyllabic and agglutinative; it encompasses the dialects and inflections, rhythms and tonalities of recorded human speech from Austro-Asiatic to Zulu-Kaffiresque. Further, it partakes of all the etymons of the animal kingdom from Aardvark to Zebra, as well as of the Avian and Piscine orders, not to say of the Cosmos. Small wonder the most patient parrot can hope to teach his friend at best no more than a rude *patois* of this language.

The discipline begins with the teacher perched on the shoulder of his pupil-friend. He sits the pupil down in a dark room, so there will be no distractions, and slowly, distinctly, for hour upon hour he repeats the primal parrot sounds. No squawks or screeches in this *séance*, nothing rancorous or raucous: rather the smaller nest noises of the forest, clucks and raspings of content and discontent, chirps and croakings simple enough for

the raw human voice to copy.

If several dozen lessons are passed to the teacher's satisfaction, a sweet enchantment sets in. The pupil gains a giddy confidence. Soon the ceremonial chittering of a parrot biting into an apple issues from his slackened mouth. Lost in a parrot trance, the pupil proceeds to early courtship chatter, minor nest-building signals, wee burbles in the forest rain. His mouth discovers rapturous new involvements for the tongue and cheek and lips; his larynx, uvula, salivary ducts, and by degrees his very tonsils are given over to medleys of puffing, popping, kissing, kvetching parrot speech. And should he be extraordinarily favored by his teacher, extraordinarily fortunate in his trance, the pupil—virtually a disciple now—will speak fluently in the mystic tongue-click language which long ago the Parrot taught the apricot-skinned Bushman nomads who wander the Kalahari Desert in faraway Botswanaland. The parrot friends vouchsafed this honor can be counted on the fingers of one hand.

SURELY A FINGER will count the name of the Most Noble Hastings Sackville Russel, twelfth Duke of Bedford. The Parrot never had a better friend. His Grace, the Duke, maintained leafy parks and aviaries at Woburn Abbey, England. His Grace raised hundreds of parrots and parrotlike birds such as the Budgerigar—that spunky Australian parakeet who is quite the rage among the British, who have nicknamed him "Budgie." His Grace studied those birds all his life and put what he learned into a book which is respected by parrot fanciers—to use the fancy name for them—the world around. His Grace loved his birds so dearly that he actually gave his life for them. He was defending a flock of Budgerigars from a predatory Sparrowhawk, when his shotgun misfired and knocked him dead, aged sixty-five, into a bush at his estate near Tavistock.

Alas, his Grace. The Duke of Bedford was the last of Britain's great parrot-fancying aristocracy. The old traditions are crumbling. To keep up a decent aviary these days will cost you plenty, and

British taxes being what they are, a peer of the realm is lucky if he can afford to keep a Budgie in a shoebox.

Old traditions are crumbling—and yet, and yet, Britain's reigning Queen Elizabeth is a Budgie enthusiast. There are said to be aviaries still at Windsor Castle, but nothing like the old days. When Elizabeth was a little girl, her grandpapa, King George V, kept a cockatoo in his bathroom, which bit up the royal bathtowels—to Queen Mary's distress. Life used to be easier for dukes and kings, as the Parrot well remembers, because he honored with his presence the Houses of Tudor and Stuart too. Henry VIII had his pet parrot and Charles II gave a parrot as a present to his girlfriend, the lovely Duchess of Richmond.

Meanwhile, over in France, in the House of Bourbon, King Louis XVI was giving parrots to his girlfriends at the same time as his Queen, Marie Antoinette, was giving parrots to her boyfriends. The birds had too much self-respect to be used as tokens in this game of royal decadence. They took to flying through the palace of Versailles with a raucous squawking that spread scandal and consternation in the court and acutely demoralized the monarchy. The parrots' indignant act was a little-known but precipitating factor in the outbreak of the French Revolution and the birth of democracy in France.

T HE PARROT has watched Man in his folly the way he watched the Brontosaurus devour the trees—with curiosity. But Man has stuck it out longer on the planet than the Thunder Lizard did, and the Parrot has developed a tolerant affection for the two-footed, wingless schmuck whose record of prolonged calamity we call History. The Parrot is no name dropper, but the fact is he has known not a few historical personages and cultural movers and shakers.

The priest-kings of the Incas and Aztecs, Manco Capac and Montezuma, adorned their heads with parrot feathers. Columbus and then the Conquistadors brought back jungle-green parrots and flamboyant red and blue macaws to delight the Queen of Spain. The silk-gowned mandarins of China sipped their tea while parrots perched upon their sleeves. The Roman emperors—the demented Nero most of all—were intrigued by the African Gray who attended their banquets and chatted with the debauched guests in Caesar's Latin. The poet Ovid mourned the death of one of these imperial birds in an elegy composed in dactylic hexameters and pentameters of incomparable perfection. Earlier still, in Greece, the parrots of Alexander the Great had of course already made friends with Aristotle. And seafaring Jews of Old Testament time—Jonah might have been among them—sailed from the Mediterranean Sea through the Pillars of Hercules and south along the African shore to the land of Ophir and returned with caged parrots to grace the palaces of King Solomon.

NOW WE HAVE TRACED the Parrot all the way back to the Bible. I have saved for the last some information about the most important person the Parrot ever knew, who was Noah. By the time Almighty God in His wrath decided to destroy His sinful creatures with the Flood, Noah was six hundred years old. Even by the Parrot's standards Noah was old. When God told Noah to build the Ark and save his family together with a male and female of every flying, walking, and creeping thing of earth, this was a tremendous responsibility for the old man. There were rumors that under the strain of it Noah had taken to drinking too much wine. Noah was the first person the Parrot had really liked. The Parrot felt sorry for his friend and wanted to help him. This is what happened.

After the Flood ended and the waters were abating from the face of the earth, after the Ark was grounded on top of Mount Ararat, Noah sent the Dove to bring back proof the land was dry once more. When the Dove came back with an olive leaf,

Noah said, "Big deal. What good's an olive leaf?" A leaf from an olive tree that grew *above* the land was not proof enough for Noah that there really was dry land out there. "You're some stupid Dove," said Noah, who was overwrought and unjustly blamed the Dove. The Parrot liked the Dove. She was pretty with her dove eyes and very ideallistic. Unfortunately, when it came to practical matters, she was something of a chucklehead. The Parrot knew there must be some better evidence there was dry land somewhere beyond the waters. So the Parrot said to Noah, "Noah, I'll take care of it," and before the old man could stop him, he flew out the window of the Ark.

Why this story was omitted from the Book of Genesis I cannot guess. I only know the parrots tell it; so it must be true. The Parrot was gone seven days and seven nights, and on the eighth day in the morning he returned with a roasted peanut in his beak. Noah knew at once there was dry land, because peanuts grow on vines and the vines spread over the dry earth. He knew at once there was dry

wood too on the dry land, because you had to rub two dry sticks together to make a fire to roast a peanut on. Tears of relief and gratitude poured down the old man's cheeks. "Parrot," he sobbed. "My dear, dear Parrot! How glad I am!"

If you don't believe this story, please close your eyes and just imagine how the Parrot must have appeared to Noah that eighth morning:

A speck coming closer and closer over the distant waters; jungle-green plumage or gray—or crimson or yellow or blue, choose your own color—and swift-beating wings coming closer and closer until Noah could see the peanut in the beak and the pleasant, amiable, comical face unique among birds to the Parrot, and he could see the parrot wink of the parrot eye with its black pupil dilating psychedelically and cheerfully in a display for his friend Noah.

"Dear Parrot. Dear, dear Parrot," was all the old man could say, over and over through his tears. The bird flew onto his shoulder and offered the peanut. Noah ate the nut slowly, the first he had

tasted in months. Fragments of the broken shell
stuck in the old man's beard and the Parrot deli-
cately preened them away.

Designed by Katy Homans

Typeset by Michael & Winifred Bixler

in Monotype Van Dijck.